THE WHISKY WAR IN ADRIAN;

OR,

The Trials and Triumphs of Prohibition

IN

LENAWEE COUNTY, MICH.

A DISCOURSE DELIVERED AT THE M. E. CHURCH IN ADRIAN, MICHIGAN, JULY 17, 1870,

BY

REV. J. S. SMART.

PUBLISHED AND ON SALE BY
J. M. ARNOLD & CO
DETROIT, MICH.

TO THE READER.

It may be considered hardly in good taste for the writer to refer to himself so frequently as he does in the following pages. His only apology is, that his position, and the part he bore in this contest have been so often, and so outrageously misrepresented, that he deemed it a duty to himself, and to his friends, to make a frank statement of his connection with the matters under discussion. He has done so, and the public, he trusts, will have the candor not to charge to egotism that which is only designed for honest self-defence. The statements are all true, and ought to be made, and should they really involve a little egotism, the generous reader will forgive that under the circumstances.

DISCOURSE.

"Woe unto him that giveth his neighbor drink, that puttest thy bottle to him and makest him drunken also."—HAB. 2, 15

"Let every soul be subject unto the higher powers. For there is no power but of God: the powers that be are ordained of God. Whosoever therefore resisteth the power, resisteth the ordinance of God: and they that resist shall receive to themselves damnation.

For rulers are not a terror to good works, but to the evil. Wilt thou then not be afraid of the power? Do that which is good, and thou shalt have praise of the same.

For he is a minister of God to thee for good. But if thou do that which is evil, be afraid; for he beareth not the sword in vain: for he is the minister of God, a revenger to execute wrath upon him that doeth evil.

Wherefore ye must needs be subject, not only for wrath, but also for conscience' sake."—ROM. 13, 1-5.

FIRST APPEARANCE OF THE ENEMY.

When I came into this city in September, 1868, one of the first disagreeable sights I saw was a staggering, reeling, drunken man on the street. My attention was called to him by a gentleman who, though professing to be a temperance man, has, so far as I know, opposed every measure to promote temperance and the enforcement of the law prohibiting the sale of liquors from that day to this. He informed me that this drunken man was a relative, that he had done much to reform him, that he had not been intoxicated before for months, and said that he could hardly abstain from cursing the men who had tempted him to his ruin. I sympathised with him. I had seen some of my own dearest friends fill drunkard's graves, and others were on the way there. I had seen the effect of intemperance in all forms of domestic misery and vice, and I could not but feel that if a man ever had cause for cursing, it was to curse the man that put the bottle to his neighbor's lips and made him drunken.

WAR DECLARED.

Not long after, I felt it my duty to preach upon the subject of temperance. My theme was "The Hell of the Heart." I endeavored to show how intemperance drowns patriotism and philanthropy, and burns out all the amiable and lovely instincts of the heart; how for the dearest and sweetest conjugal affection, it substitutes infidelity, morose bestiality, heartless cruelty, demoniacal tyranny and hate; how it expels the most tender parental love, and makes an otherwise kind and generous father a robber, a pest, and a terror in his own home; how it places Satan on the throne of God, and makes the heaven of the heart a burning, seething pit of woe, where shame, gloom, terror, rage, sorrow, anguish, remorse, despair, form so many flames of that hell the smoke of whose torment ascendeth up for ever and ever. I made the most earnest appeal I possibly could to drinkers to dissuade them from their cups. Previous to the delivery of this sermon I had visited most of the saloons in the city, giving notice of the theme I intended to discuss, and inviting both saloon-keepers and drinkers to come and hear for themselves. But the work of drunkard-making still went on. I scarcely ever went, in the after part of the day, from my house on Toledo street, down on Main to Maumee street, without seeing more or less drooling, staggering, lounging, idiotic drunkenness. Thank God, there is less now than there was then.

A False Position.

Not many months had passed when a convention was held at Jackson to organize a Temperance Political Party. Being busy in revival work at home, I did not attend it. My absence from this convention was made an occasion of putting me in a position of antagonism to the new party, through an article appearing editorially in the *Adrian Times*, but written by a prominent member of my own church. As I did not desire to occupy that position before the public, I, in the most courteous language at my command, corrected the mistake, saying that when I thought it would be of advantage to the public to know my political status, I would define my own position. In a private conversation I assured the editor at the same time that I allowed no man to take possession of me or of my political principles; that, while I resided in Adrian, no man would be authorized to speak for me upon such subjects. Being of age, I preferred to speak for myself. This being communicated to the writer of the article, gave, as I afterwards learned, very grave offense.

An Attack from Behind Intrenchments.

In the same issue of the *Times* the Good Templars, who were doing more to keep alive temperance agitation and temperance sentiment than all other agencies outside of the churches, were severely assailed by an anonymous writer for not admitting colored people to membership, and two of the local pastors were arraigned and charged with great inconsistency for belonging to such an association, as they were known to be abolitionists. Not knowing or suspecting who wrote the article, I, unfortunately, fell in company with its author, and denounced it in his presence as the work of some meddling scribbler who was, evidently, very anxious to write, and who was entirely unworthy of notice, and remarked that the ministers in question would be very foolish to give it any public attention. I am of the same opinion still, but might not have expressed myself quite so freely had I known that I was in the presence of the writer. A stranger who freely criticizes an anonymous writer is like a man walking barefooted in the Dismal Swamp. He knows not how soon he may tread upon a serpent who will curl and bite.

It is of doubtful morality, and of more doubtful courage, to make personal assaults in anonymous communications. To strike a man who is exposed and off his guard from behind a cover where you cannot be seen, is hardly doing as you would be done by, to say the least. Anonymous writers, therefore, who deal in gross personalities, ought not to be too sensitive if they should be severely criticized, even in their own presence. Whatever the design of this attack might have been, or to whomsoever it might have been aimed, or whatever the motive that prompted it, the effect of it was to divert the attention of the public from the question of temperance, and in some measure to draw off the Good Templars from their legitimate work to attend a newspaper discussion, which degenerated into a not very reputable personal squabble between the attacking party and one of the clergymen in question.

Victims.

In the meantime the work of moral degradation and death was going on in the city and county. One man had, in a drunken fit, been strangled to death on our streets, another in a neighboring town had been murdered in a fit of intoxication by his son-in-law, others were occasionally dying with the delirium tremens, and not a few of our best families were seeing their most promising sons entering upon a course of infamy and wretchedness under the influence of saloons, licensed contrary to the constitution and statute of the State, to drag them down to the drunkard's doom.

Recruiting Officers.

We had at this time in this city, forty-six of these drunkard making establishments, and about one hundred in the County, receiving the bodies and souls of men at an expense of not less than $300,000 per year.

Second Assault upon the Enemy's Works.

Under these circumstances, I thought it my duty to preach upon the criminality of the liquor-selling business, and the relation of intemperance to crime in general.

In this sermon I endeavored to show that this business was of itself, and according to the law of the State, one of perpetual crime inality, and that the City Council, to the extent of the influence of its license, was accessory to it, and responsible for it. A great excitement followed.

The Enemy again Behind Intrenchments.

I was severely criticized by an anonymous writer in the *Times*, and more light upon various points was called for. Special fault was found with the attack I had made upon the Council, and its illegal license system. I made no defense through the press, but merely published that portion of my sermon which had been made the subject of special criticism. This was reviewed by Dr. Charles Rynd, the reputed author, and most prominent advocate of our now exploded municipal license system, over his own proper name.

Third Assault on the Enemy.

I preached another sermon on the Sunday evening following, on the relation of the liquor traffic to the crime of murder, demonstrating that nine-tenths of all assaults and batteries, manslaughters and murders are the result of this business, and giving the light called for upon other points in controversy.

Licenses Reduced.

During the week the licenses were reduced to five dollars, and a prohibitory clause incorporated into them, so that the text of the license might not be in direct contradiction to the law of the State. As these licenses were worthless, it was thought best not to charge much for them. They could not be used in courts of law to befog the minds of susceptible jurors, as the old license had been. Their moral support in this form might be worth a trifle, but not much.

Moving Directly upon the Enemy's Works.

About this time some of our citizens took measures to enforce the prohibitory law with renewed energy. From January 1st to July 10th, 1869, twenty-four suits had been brought for violation of the prohibitory law. The cases complained of were all of an aggravated character. The first two were in behalf of a poor woman whose husband had been reformed by the Good Templars, and had joined the lodge, but was tempted to drink again in the saloons, and by his drunkenness not only disgraced the lodge, but brought his family into great distress. It was at the earnest entreaty of his suffering wife that the suits were brought. The next two were precisely of the same character. The next two were brought in behalf of a distressed family, where a young man had been put in jail for (in a fit of intoxication) beating his mother. This young man had been a Good Templar, and great efforts had been made to reform him. He had a good education, and might have made a useful member of society. He wrote me a letter from the jail, which was one of the most touching appeals for sympathy and aid that I ever read. I visited him in jail, and there he pleaded with me, with tears, and with the most earnest vows of reformation, to help him. Some of his friends bailed him out, and used him as a witness against those who had ruined him. But he soon fell into their toils again, and I never shall forget the look of wild despair which he gave me when the Sheriff was about to take him to the House of Correction in Detroit, and I told him I could not help him. He leaped from the cars under full motion on their way to Detroit, and got safely away. I have since heard, though I know not whether it be true, that he is dead. The next two cases were in behalf of Good Templars, who were reformed drunkards, and had fallen again under the enticements of these drunkard-making establishments, and had been sent to jail in consequence. The next two were in behalf of the woman who first complained on account of her husband. She was in great distress, and sought—as she had a right to do—the protection of the laws. The next two were for selling to two young boys whose mothers came and, with tears, entreated that the shield of the law might be thrown over their children. The next two were in behalf of a woman who had been reduced to almost a starving condition on account of the drunkenness of her husband, having nothing for herself and her little ones to eat but potatoes when the complaint was made. He was a fine mechanic, and a kind, generous husband and father when sober. Out of the twenty-four cases eighteen were successful, and every one of them was similar to the above, with the single exception of one, where the saloon keeper dared Mr. Van Sandt to prosecute him, and he accepted the challenge. We invoked the protection of the law in behalf of tempted virtue, in behalf of children at the earnest request of weeping mothers, in behalf of wives and children driven to despair, and almost to starvation, through the drunkenness of their natural protectors and providers, and tried to arrest the blow of the infuriated wretch who would beat his own mother, and for this we were branded as fanatics and disturbers of the peace!

The Whisky Ring.

A whisky ring was organized which had its secret meetings, and took measures to resist these so-called indiscriminate prosecutions. A common fund was raised, and oaths and obligations bound these bad men into a sort of infernal brotherhood. The members of this ring felt that they were at the heart of a great social and commercial, and political power, and desired nothing so much as to throw their hot blood through the whole body of their sympathizers. They thought, if they could mass their forces, they could by threats, and acts of violence, financial pressure, social and political influence, and mob law, intimidate the law-abiding citizens, and crush out the authority of the State.

Hotels and Saloons Closed.

Accordingly, on the morning of the 12th of July, 1869, the hotels, making common cause with the saloons, closed. They declared that, if they could not be allowed to sell intoxicating liquors in peace, they would ruin the business of the city.

Travelers were thrown upon the streets without hotel accommodations, and the saloon-keepers were lounging around the street corners to see how the trick would work. The business of the city could not, of course, flow in its ordinary channels without hotel accommodations, and the hotel keepers expected that the great mass of the business men would at once demand that they should open again, and would agree to protect the saloons against any further prosecutions. Such was the state of affairs when, about half-past one o'clock P. M., I had occasion to go down to the post office. I found considerable excitement, and at least a hundred men gathered in front of the post office, in earnest, if not angry discussion. Travelers were clamoring for places of entertainment, temperance men were accusing liquor sellers with perjury to shield their criminal business, and liquor sellers were cursing the law, and every body that sustained it. I saw in this crowd what I felt possibly might be an incipient riot. Let the first blow be struck, or the first shot be fired, and no man could tell the consequences. I instantly determined to cut the knot and relieve the case. I consulted rapidly with a number of citizens about the propriety of calling a public meeting, stepped into a store, wrote a hand bill, calling a meeting of law-and-order citizens to make provision for the traveling public, took it to the Times Office, ordered five hundred copies to be printed and distributed forthwith and charged to me.

First Public Meeting of the Friends of Law and Order.

Accordingly, at five o'clock a meeting assembled at Odd Fellows' Hall. James Berry, Esq., was called to the chair, and Prof. J. W. McKeever was elected secretary. A committee of five ladies, consisting of Mrs. Peters, Mrs. Young, Mrs. Burlingame, Mrs. James

Berry and Mrs. E. Van Sandt, was appointed to canvass for places to accommodate travelers. Messrs. Fairbanks, A. B. Palmer and E. Van Sandt, were appointed a committee to direct travelers to places of entertainment. James Berry, Esq., W. S. Wilcox, Esq., Josiah Rowley, Esq. and Dr. H. Knapp were appointed a committee to take a general oversight of affairs, to inquire into the expediency of establishing a temperance hotel, and to make such other provision for the traveling public as might be necessary, with power to call future public meetings, etc., etc. All these committees addressed themselves immediately to their work, and in two hours the traveling public was provided for, an ample hotel having been opened, founded upon the hospitality of the citizens, with office and hack book, and sample room for agents, on Maumee street, in the very centre of the business of the city, with hacks and omnibuses running regularly to and from the cars, and a clerk to distribute guests to their homes, and thus the train which had been laid to blow up the city was beautifully and effectually cut. This movement took the whisky men by surprise. They did not expect it, and hardly knew how to meet it.

The Efforts of the Enemy to Destroy the Business of the City.

But their plan was to injure the business of the city, if possible. The hotels made their strike in the time of year when very little business is done at any rate, as the farmers are very busy in their harvest fields. All the dullness in general business was persistently attributed to the closing of the saloons. We were told that grass would grow in the streets if the saloons were not opened. This cry, started by the saloon keepers, was taken up by their thirsty friends, and finally adopted by many very respectable people, who, I suppose, really believed that the liquor traffic, which always tends to pauperism and crime, was necessary to the good order and prosperity of society. If the business ot the city was not injured, it was not the fault of the saloon keepers or their friends. They did the best they could to injure it. It is said that they circulated stories in every direction through the adjacent country to the effect that the small pox was raging fearfully in the city, and that they really stopped teams on their way to Adrian by these alarming representations. They threatened to take lives, burn buildings, and destroy property generally, and alarmed a great many good men. They had determined to compel the public to sanction and protect their infamous traffic. To use the language of the Common Council, they virtually said:

"Allow us to sell liquors in violation of the law of the State, and protect us therein, or we will to the best of our ability, destroy the the business of the city." This attitude is sufficient to indicate the desperate character of the men. Every citizen with the spirit of a man in him, should have met them with prompt and open defiance. When men of this character are met bravely, they seldom do mischief, but the moment you show symptoms of fear, and cower before them, you are in danger. It was truly amusing to see how many quaked and trembled, and by their spirit and conversation really encouraged the desperate measures of these reckless men.

Burning the Imerson House.

In the meantime the committee appointed for the purpose had rented the Imerson House for a temperance hotel, and expected to open it on Saturday the 17th. But on Saturday morning about three o'clock, the city was aroused by an alarm of fire. The Imerson House was burned.

Second Public Meeting of the Friends of Law and Order.

The committee immediately issued a call for another public meeting at Odd Fellows' Hall, on Saturday afternoon. The meeting being called to order, a committe on resolutions was appointed, consisting of Messrs. Josiah Rowley, D. D. Sinclair, and W. S. Wilcox. The committee appointed at the previous meeting, July 12th, reported progress. They had associated with themselves Messrs. D. D. Sinclair, J. R. McEldowney, H. S. Russell, C. E. Weaver and J. W. McKeever. They had visited the hotels for the purpose of prevailing upon the proprietors to open their houses, and secured a promise from Mr. Wheeler, of the Botsford Hotel, to open on Wednesday, which however he failed to do. Remarks were made by several gentlemen on the state of the city, the propriety of enforcing the law, etc., when Mr. James Berry called attention to the object of the meeting. He said the object of the meeting was to take steps to provide for the accommodation of travelers. Should we allow men to hold a club over our heads and threaten to injure us? The committee had rented a hotel, the liquor men had fired it. That, as he understood it, was a notice to quit. If we rent another we shall receive a similar notice to quit. The committee ask for instructions. The committee on resolutions here reported the following:

RESOLVED, That one part of our business here to-day is to promote the good order of society, and the peaceful enforcement of the laws of the land. If the laws be allowed to be trampled under foot, and the city be surrendered to the hands of an association conspiring against law, no law-abiding citizen can be safe. All our rights, our property, and our lives themselves will be at the mercy of wicked and reckless men, It is the duty, therefore, of every good citizen to pledge his all, if need be, to sustain the enforcement of law.

RESOLVED, That the committees appointed by the public meeting held on Monday last, by their prompt, discreet and energetic action in making all the necessary arrangements to relieve the business of the city from any serious embarrassment in consequence of the sudden closing of the hotels, and to preserve the peace and good order of the city, are deserving of the most earnest gratitude not only of temperance men, but of every law-abiding citizen.

RESOLVED, That the hotels, by making common cause with the saloons, and, without notice to the public, suddenly closing, embarrassing travel, distinctly and professedly aiming a blow at the general business and prosperity of the city, have done great injustice to the traveling public and to the business community at large, and upon them rests the responsibility solely of our present difficulties."

These resolutions having been adopted, a committee was ordered to raise funds to pay expenses, and the Common Council was requested to increase the night police force of the city. The committee having general charge of affairs was instructed to add to its numbers, and go on with its work, meeting emergencies as they might arise.

STATE OF THE PUBLIC MIND AFTER THE FIRE.

The law and order men adopted all necessary precautions to defend themselves against personal violence, or other injuries threatened by the lawless characters who were endeavoring by force to control the city. A secret police was organized, and every point of danger was thoroughly guarded. I have no doubt but the leaders of the conspiracy did their utmost to keep things quiet after the fire. They felt that they had possibly gone a little too far. I think they feared the law-and-order men, and they had reason to, for they were very firm and determined. The saloon men and hotel keepers certainly feared each other, and they had reason to, for they were desperate characters. And it is useless to deny that the temperance men feared the liquor men, for they knew that they were encouraged in their desperate measures by many of the most wealthy and influential men in the city. This wholesome dread all around did much, I have no doubt, to preserve the peace, and so perfectly was the peace preserved, that there was not, I think, a blow struck, or a public brawl of any kind in the city while the saloons were closed. Some went out of the city limits and got drunk, and had some fighting among themselves, I believe, just by way of recreation. This was their way of keeping the Sabbath. But the city itself was probably never so quiet for the same length of time before. The hotels and saloons had now been closed a week. Some of our citizens had seen the first sober week they had enjoyed for years. Many a drunkard's wife had begun to rejoice once more in a sober husband, and a peaceful home, and none but God can tell how many prayed, and what agonizing prayers were offered that the saloons might never open again. But every body was cursing the hotels. It was every way to them a losing business. Their rents went on; their taxes had to be paid; they could not discharge all their help. Doing nothing was not a money making business. They were not only losing money, but friends. Degraded to the level of the lowest groggeries in the city, they stood there in the eye of the public which had pampered and enriched them, as great ghostly monuments of ingratitude and folly. I ought to have mentioned that immediately after the burning of the Imerson House, the elder Sammons broke from the ring and opened his hotel. He was severely threatened, but his property was well guarded, and no mischief ensued. It was also understood that the reason why the Botsford Hotel did not open, was because the landlord did not dare to meet the threats of his desperate associates. He desired to open, but they would not allow it. They were still determined to hold the lash over the city, till it should come down upon its knees and surrender to them. They proposed to show that they were the masters, and that the thirsty citizens were their abject slaves. They had not yet accomplished their purpose. What was to be done? There were plenty of men craven enough to acknowledge their authority, and to tell them that the law of the State was odious and impracticable, and could not be enforced, and all that, but that, though very good aid and comfort as far as it went, was not enough. They demanded some more formal endorsement and guaranty of protection. How to secure these was not yet apparent.

The Enemy in Council at the Opera House.

At last it was concluded, on Monday, the 19th, to call a great public meeting at the Opera Hall, in their interest. What to do? To give the hotels and saloons permission to open? Who closed them? Nobody. They closed voluntarily. Could anything be more degrading than to submit to the tyranny of their lash, and beg them to open under the circumstances? Could anything be more infamous than to assemble at their dictation to trample upon the authority of the State? A few of the saloons had been prosecuted to save suffering wives from the brutality of drunken husbands, to protect the prostrate mother from the murderous blows of an inebriated son, to throw the shield of law over children tempted to their ruin. And these guilty men had now conspired to ruin the business of the city, and had begun to burn the property of honest, law abiding citizens. It was in sympathy with such characters, and with their accursed work that this meeting was called, and to the shame of the city be it said, though the rain poured down in torrents when it was assembling, it was really a large meeting, numerously attended by men of wealth and high social position. After due deliberation, this great meeting passed the following:

"Whereas, There is now a great antagonism existing in our city, upon the subject of keeping hotels and saloons open; And whereas, this feeling has culminated in a great crime, that of arson; And whereas, we are satisfied, that until the nature of man is changed, while part of community will insist on dictating morals, and the pursuit of business to the other part, that such outrages will not cease; therefore,

Resolved, That we believe it for the best interest of our city, that every man mind his own business, and let his neighbor's alone.

Resolved, That should our hotel and saloon keepers resume their occupations, and conduct their business in an orderly manner, that we believe it would be for the best interest of our city to let them alone."

Let us look at this production a moment. Its literary character speaks for itself, but that is of no consequence. What we are interested in is the sentiment which it contains. We are told that "there is now a great antagonism in our city upon the subject of keeping hotels and saloons open." What was the nature of this "antagonism?" Did any body oppose the keeping open of the hotels? Certainly, the law-and-order men did not. They had been to the hotel keepers, and expostulated with them for closing. At great inconvenience they were making hotels of their own homes to provide for the traveling public, which it was the duty of the regular hotels to entertain. And as to the saloons, had they not a perfect right to close in obedience to the law of the State, if they wished to? Who had the right to antagonize their will in this respect? Had they not done right in closing, and whose business was it? Who had a right to find fault with men in their first efforts to obey the laws of the State? Certainly, law abiding citizens had no right to find fault, and they did not. Where was the "antagonism?" The hotel men had attempted to bully the city, and had not thus far succeeded very well. They and their friends were not well satisfied with their success. They had declared open war upon the prosperity of the city. That naturally engendered a feeling of opposition, but who was to blame for it? Nobody but themselves. We are told again that "this feeling has already culminated in a great crime; that of arson." Who was to blame for that? The law-and-order men were honestly, industriously and peaceably providing for the traveling public. They were working hard and making no little sacrifice to promote the prosperity of the city. But those who had declared war upon its prosperity, the enemies of the public, had burned the hotel that the law abiding citizens were about to open. But in all this great meeting, there was not one word of censure for these vile incendiaries, or for their crime. But we are warned that upon certain conditions, "such outrages will not cease." What are the conditions upon which the execution of this threat depends? "While part of community will insist on dictating morals, and the pursuit of business to the other part." This certainly is a very remarkable sentence. Can these gentlemen tell us in what part of the world this is not done? What would that government be which did not dictate morals? Is it wrong for the virtuous public to legislate against murder, manslaughter, adultery, bigamy, theft, burglary, fraud, perjury? Is it wrong for good citizens to enforce the laws against these offences? And will men who have property and lives, and domestic virtue and happiness to be protected, threaten arson if such laws are enforced? But why not? This is "dictating morals and the pursuit of business." Suppose a number of persons in our community should open an establishment for counterfeiting, and another for selling foreign goods that had not paid the duty, and the law should be enforced against them, and they should in retaliation burn your house, or burn down a legal banking house, or a store where business was conducted according to law, what would you think of the men that would threaten a continuance of such outrages, "while part of community will insist on dictating morals, and the pursuit of business to the other part?" But counterfeiting and smuggling are not as bad as drunkard making. The cases are entirely analagous. Because the law was enforced against some very aggravated cases of drunkard making, the hotels connected with this illegal business closed, and when other citizens attempted to open a hotel, to be conducted according to law, it was burned. Then a great meeting of prominent citizens assemble, and in a threatening manner intimates that if we interfere with the illegal business of these drunkard makers and incendiaries, we may expect more of the same thing. These men, who live upon the miseries, and minister to the worst vices of society, who would debauch your innocent child, or thrust your gray-haired father drunken into perdition, who trample upon all law both human and divine, who would take your life, or burn your house over your head, are virtually endorsed and encouraged to sustain their business by arson, and kindred offences, and that, too, by a large number of the business men of the city. What do these men mean? Do they not themselves need the protection of the laws? When they once put the torch into the hand of the incendiary, and say to him, "Go, burn!" are they quite sure that he will use the fire discreetly? Is it not possible that it may find way to their property? These are dangerous characters to cultivate. When man begin to trample upon good and wholesome laws, and defy the law making power, they know not when to stop. Is it not astonishing that men of wealth and high social position, should not only condemn the enforcement of the laws, but should tacitly sanction and encourage crimes like arson, to break down the authority of the State? Certainly, men who will deliberately take such measures, do not themselves deserve the protection of the laws, and if every one of these men had found their houses in flames before the next morning, it would have been but the logical result of their own teaching.

Before the chief speaker upon this occasion had finished his speech, he began himself to dictate morals. "He thought the right way of dealing with this question was to punish the drunkard. That might lead him to reflect on the error of his ways. It might have a tendency to reform him." "Dictating morals!" He said, "He believed in the enforcement of the liquor law in some cases." "The pursuit of business!" But the cases wherein the liquor law had been enforced were just such as those in which he himself says that he would enforce the law. These gentlemen tell us that they "believe it for the best interest of the city that every man mind his own business, and let his neighbor's alone." Why did not they do so? Why did not they act as they believed? Were they minding their own business when they assembled together to sanction and encourage liquor selling and house burning? They were not liquor sellers. What had they to do with fostering up an illegal business? What business was it to them who enforced the laws of the State? Their whole meeting was one grand impertinence, attending to matters that were none of their business. The truth is, it is every good citizens' business to obey the laws of the land, and to aid in their enforcement. When men are doing so, those who interfere to prevent it, are attending to that which is none of their business. What right, according to their principle, have they to dictate that the saloon keepers shall "conduct their business in an orderly manner?" I thought every man was to attend to his own business, and to let his neighbor's alone. The truth is, this cannot be. Every man is responsible to society for the character of his business, as well as for the manner in which it is conducted. No man has a right to engage in a business which is generally injurious to society, and these gentlemen know it just as well as we do. How did the law-and-order men meet this remarkable manifesto? How did they meet the threats of continued house burning? They met them with the firmness and calm dignity which had characterized all their acts.

Law and Order Men in Council at the Opera House.

They assembled on the 21st of July at the Opera House, James Berry, Esq., presiding, and Prof. J. W. McKeever, acting secretary, and adopted the following:

Resolved, That we seek all our objects in a peaceful and legal way, and most earnestly protest against the incendiarism threatened in the resolutions passed by the friends of the liquor traffic, on Monday last, in their meeting, that if the laws are enforced, outrages like arson will not cease, and assure those who make such threats that they cannot thus intimidate the friends of law and order, or turn them from their purpose."

Thus the two parties squarely faced each other, the one standing on whisky and arson, the other on temperance and law. Rev. John Russell, of the Peninsular Herald, was present, and made an able address. Among other things, he said, "We are minding our own business when we are taking care of the interests of society. The second resolution (passed by the friends of the liquor traffic,) is correct, if properly understood. If the hotel and saloon keepers should resume their business, and conduct it in an orderly way, they should be let alone, but selling liquor contrary to law is not orderly. They should sell legitimate things, and then they would be let alone. If they keep liquor for sale, they are not orderly, and they should not be let alone. But the preamble is the worst part of this report. Of course this antagonism should cease, but not by the law-and-order men submitting to wrong. They have not been unkind, but have acted impartially. The side which is wrong should cease its wrong doing, and then all antagonism will cease. The law is for the lawless and disobedient, and resistance to it is wrong. The rebels only asked to be let alone, but we told them they must submit to law, even as we did ourselves. So we say to the liquor sellers. We ask nothing more of them than we are willing to submit to ourselves. These men voluntarily violate law, and then because they are prosecuted for it, the hotels make common cause with them, and attempt to injure the business of the city. Then they cooly turn to us, who are law-abiding citizens, and say, his contest ought to stop. You men of law and order should take your hands off. Suppose we should to-night enter the house of the President of this meeting for purposes of robbery, and he should resist us, how would it sound to him for us to say, 'This antagonism must stop; you are stirring up a great deal of bad feeling; you ought to submit.' It is the man who is violating law who should cease his antagonism.

The preamble says, this has culminated in arson. This refers to the burning of the Imerson House. Who did that? Was it the temperance men that burned their own house? No one believes it. This document says while one part of the community insists upon dictating morals, and the pursuit of business to another part, these outrages will not cease. Did they really mean this? Did they really mean to declare what may be logically inferred from this preamble, that is, that they are guilty of burning the Imerson House, and they will continue to burn unless the enforcement of the law be stopped? Let such a sentiment be rebuked by the community. You cannot do less than to pass this resolution." He said he could not believe that the gentlemen who adopted this report intended all that this preamble intimated. He thought they must have adopted it ignorantly or hastily, not realizing what they were doing. I think he was right, for the liquor sellers themselves were disgusted with it, and I doubt if any man voted for it who was not ashamed of his act in thirty minutes afterwards. It satisfied nobody, and I doubt if any man ever seriously defended it after the meeting adjourned. The saloon keepers thought this would hardly do to open under. They desired a more respectable endorsement. The temperance men were still masters of the situation. What was to be done next? They had nothing to do, of course, but to wait and watch until the enemies of the law should make another move.

The Great Petition.

If you want to get anything done that is really infamous, the easiest way to do it is to draw up a petition skillfully, and long enough so that no one will desire to take the trouble of reading it through, putting the specially objectionable points well down in the body of the document, and then have it circulated by a smooth talking respectable gentleman, who shall go to his neighbors alone, and without discussing the merits of the matter involved in it, apply for signatures, and many a man would give his name to a petition to hang his own mother, and never know the difference till the rope was round her neck.

It is not strange that a petition should be the last resort in this bill of abominations. This would succeed when everything else would fail. But to whom should it be addressed? The only body having any authority in the premises was a State Constitutional Convention or the Legislature, and then the voting population of the whole State. There was no legitimate relief for the dram shops, except in a change of the Constitution and the Statute of the State. But the Common Council by its former license policy, had in effect, set aside the Constitution and the Laws. Some of the same men were in the Council now, and others that were no better. Might they not be tempted to do the same thing, if sufficient outside pressure were brought to bear upon them? The moral effect of a petition generally signed, and published with the name of the signers boldly attached, would be very great, and a favorable opinion from the Council, which, in response to such a petition, it would have an excuse for giving, would a least add weight and dignity to the opposition. Though every man of any intelligence knew that the Council had no legal right to interfere, except to secure the enforcement of law, yet for the sake of securing the moral weight of its sanction, it was determined to appeal to it. Accordingly a petition was drawn up and put in circulation, containing among other things, the following:

"As an expression of opinion merely, your petitioners would respectfully suggest that your honorable body recommend to the persons engaged in prosecuting for violation of the Maine Law, to desist further action, and that you secure by municipal legislation, the interest of the community against evils growing out of the sale of spirituous liquors, as far as may be practicable. The restriction imposed by a former city government, with such others as may be deemed important, would, in the opinion of your petitioners, produce the results desired."

"The restriction imposed by a former city government," was simply the old license system which had been exploded and set aside by every justice of the peace and judge before whom it had come, and had been repudiated by the Council itself as unconstitutional and illegal, and therefore null and void. To "recommend to the persons engaged in prosecuting for violation of the Maine Law, to desist further action," was simply to recommend that the liquor saloons be allowed to open without molestation, and that they resume their business under the special care and protection of the city authorities. I have no idea that one person in ten, who signed this petition, ever even read this clause in it. It was put far down into the body of the document, and buried up and smothered in a mass of talk about "trade," and "business," and "excitement," and "distraction," and "animosity," and "extreme men on either side," and expressions of respect for, and laudations of the ability and power of the Common Council, and deprecations of the evils of liquor selling, and protestations of a deep interest in the welfare of the city, and other literary flourishes, enough to blind the eyes of, and deceive the very elect. But whether understood or not by the petitioners, this petition was signed by a hundred and fifty of our most prominent citizens, among whom were many members of all our Christian churches. It was entirely satisfactory to the whisky ring, and a most stunning blow to the friends of temperance and law. The liquor sellers looked upon it rightly as an endorsement of their business, and as a withering rebuke to those who had prosecuted them. Stripped of its verbiage, in plain English, it was saying to the authority of the State and to the temperance men, "Stand back gentleman, let this work of death go on. We stand by the dram shops and the whisky ring." Had this petition been couched in words like these:

"To his Honor, the Mayor, and Common Council of the City of Adrian: The undersigned citizens and business men of the city would repectfully petition you to perjure yourselves, by setting aside the Constitution and Law of the State which you are sworn to observe, and by giving your sanction to a business which has no legal right to exist, and which it is your sworn duty to suppress, and that you officially rebuke all those who are endeavoring, as good citizens, through the courts by the ordinary processes of law, in jury trials, to suppress this illegal business, and that you officially invite the saloon keepers to resume their abominable traffic, under your especial care and protection."

How many respectable men do you suppose would have signed it? Not one. Any decent man would have felt it an insult to ask his name to such a paper. The Council would have spurned such a document. But what is the difference? There is no difference except in the style; one paper is written to conceal ideas, the other to express them, but they both amount to the same thing. I have no idea that all these petitioners intended as much as this. They did not critically examine the petition, and did not realize its bearing. But the writer of it, and the saloon keepers, and the whisky ring understood it. Had it been understood by the signers generally, it would have required no small amount of courage for a man to attach his name to such a document, and have it published to the world. It is a record one would hardly like to preserve for his posterity. Had I put my name there, and should one of my children's children a hundred years hence find it, I should feel like rising from my grave to tear it from his hand, lest he should feel his blood to be tainted by it. Not so with the record of those who stood for humanity, and law, and right, in this contest. Theirs is a noble record, of which they may well be proud, and which they may bequeath to their children as a treasure more precious than gold, and which will enrich and ennoble their blood in all their generations. Remembering this, let true men take courage and never be disheartened at temporary reverses. Many, I know, were disheartened at the overwhelming social power of this last movement. When the petition was published, with the names attached, it seemed to demoralize the whole community. I preached a short time afterwards in favor of doing right rather than to consult present self-interest or policy. It was a sermon I had prepared for another occasion, dealing mostly in general principles, but I was amazed to see what a fever it stirred throughout the community. Men talked about it upon the streets the next day, as though some great outrage had been committed. One gentlemen witstood me to the face, claiming that it was a duty to do wrong when the success of your business and the support of your family depended on it, and applied his principle particularly to the signing of this petition. I do not remember to have heard any one defend this act on the ground that it was right. This was not the ground assumed by the petitioners at all. "Trade" and "business" were the great considerations pressed. Their craft was in danger. Once more to refer to the language of the Common Council, the liquor men virtually said: "Allow us to sell liquor in violation of the law of the State, and protect us therein, or we will, to the best of our ability, destroy the business of the city."

These petitioners simply echoed, "*destroy the business of the city!*" It came from them like a groan of agonizing despair. Their cry to the Council was, "don't let them do it. We submit. We know we are in their hands. We are terribly 'excited,' 'distracted,' 'filled with apprehension concerning the ultimate and permanent prosperity of the city.' Let these men sell liquor. License them. Protect them. Do anything you can to appease them. Advise the temperance men not to prosecute. Try and make the business respectable. We entreat you to stop this terrible animosity."

Can you imagine a more humiliating spectacle? The great mass of our business men absolutely subjugated, at the feet of liquor sellers and incendiaries, looking up to the City Council, crying for mercy! There is no language at my command which can express the depth of my commisseration for men in such an attitude. Only one step lower is possible, and that was reserved for the Committee on Licenses of the present Council, which proposes to pay the fines of these lawless drunkard makers out of the treasury of the city. Did these petitioners really feel that they were in the power of these men? Did they sincerely believe that the general business of the city would be ruined if the liquor traffic should never again be resumed? Did they suppose it necessary, in order to the re-opening of the saloons, that they should interpose their influence in favor of them? We had reason to know that they would open in three days, with or without the sanction of the business men, or of the Council. Did they not know it? If so, what excuse was there for this humiliating petition? Why enlarge the power of the whisky ring, by giving it the influence of a hundred and fifty of our most conspicuous names? Was it to save the liquor sellers from an occasional prosecution and fine? Was it to overawe the temperance men, and make it impossible for them to enforce the law? Was it that suffering wives and starving children, and prostrate mothers might hereafter cry to us in vain for the protection of the laws? I would rather my hand would wither from my arm forever, than to have traced my name in such a connection, and for such a purpose. I hardly have patience to argue this question of profit and loss, when interests so much higher than mere pecuniary considerations are pressing upon my mind. But as this is the great argument of the petitioners, I will devote a moment to it. The Massachusetts State Temperance Alliance has published a tract containing the following facts, which ought to be in the hands of every one of these gentlemen: "For the price of three glasses of intoxicating liquor a day, you may purchase for your family every Saturday night, the following: seven lbs. of flour, one lb. breakfast coffee, two lbs. brown sugar, one quart of beans, one-quarter lb. tea, one lb. granulated sugar, one lb. butter, one bar of soap, or four lbs. corned beef, two lbs. ham, two lbs. steak, two lbs. salt pork. Or you can buy for the year, two tons of coal, four lbs. tea, fifty lbs. granulated sugar, ten galls. molasses, two bush. of meal, one-half bush. beans, fifteen bars soap, five lbs. starch, twenty lbs. raisins, four lbs. ginger, twenty lbs. rice, two bbls. flour, twenty lbs. breakfast coffee, one hundred lbs. brown sugar, thirty lbs. butter, ten bush. potatoes, five galls. kerosene oil, five lbs. saleratus, two hundred lbs. salt fish, one lb. nutmegs, two lbs. cassia, five lbs. soda, or one hundred lbs. corned beef, forty lbs. ham, fifty lbs. salt pork, forty lbs. lard, seventy-four lbs. mutton, fifty lbs. steak, sixty lbs. fresh pork, one hundred lbs. beef for roasting, fifty lbs. sausages."

Here is an amount of legitimate trade which may be multiplied by thousands, all of which is diverted from its regular channels, and absorbed by this illegal and infamous traffic. Other articles of comfort from other branches of trade might, of course, be substituted for the above. Thus, while the drinker and his family are impoverished, every legitimate branch of trade is robbed by this vile business, and the aggregate amount is very great. The amount of money expended in fifty drinking saloons in this city, would not be less than one hundred thousand dollars per year. This one hundred thousand dollars is diverted from legitimate business channels, and sunk in these sinks of depravity and death. Would it not be better for community if this money were sunk in the depths of the sea? How is general business promoted by this waste? The legitimate business of the city is robbed of more than a hundred thousand dollars a year by the illegal traffic in strong drink. The liquor sellers cannot add to the wealth of community. They are not producers. They are the moths, leeches, blood-suckers of society. They eat out the substance of private families, and curse and wither every other branch of trade. How can a business, which every body admits produces more idleness, pauperism and crime than all other causes combined, tend to promote the prosperity of the city? Let us look at this matter. Fifty saloons will consume the time of seventy-five able bodied men to run them, will cultivate one hundred and fifty loungers and gamblers as constant attendants, will keep constantly an average of five delegates in State Prison, five in the House of Correction, five in the Lock-up or County Jail, five in the Poor House, and will kill about one a month, making about twelve a year—in all, two hundred and fifty-seven, whose time, at a dollar a day for three hundred days in the year, would be worth $67,100. The cash taken for liquor over the bar could not be less than $100,000. Then there is the expense of prosecution and keeping in Jail, Poor House, House of Correction, State Prison, etc., all of which would make the aggregate expense crowd $200,000. What good does this vast expenditure do? Is it not worse than wasted? Is it not a curse to community? Does it not rob all other branches of trade? Is it not astonishing to hear business men plead for this traffic in the name of "general business," and of the "best interests of community," and of the "permanent prosperity of the city." But it will be said that the plea was not put upon this ground, but on the ground that business would be "diverted and turned away to neighboring towns." Col. Eldredge told us, in the great Opera House meeting, "He did not believe that grass would grow in the streets of the city if the present state of affairs continued, but he did believe that Adrian would see a tremendous falling off in the trade of the city. He did not believe the farmers would come here to trade if they could get nothing to drink." This sentiment, it is true, is reiterated by the petitioners. But no matter where or by whom stated, this is but a shallow pretense which can have no foundation in truth. In the first place, the business of the farmers in Adrian does not depend upon their getting something to drink. In the next place, they would be more likely to get it, even under a rigorous enforcement of the law, in Adrian, than in any of the neighboring towns. Adrian has as many liquor shops as all the rest of the County put together. Let the law be enforced in Adrian, and you will enforce it in the "neighboring towns" without trouble. This we have proved by experiment.

What, then, becomes of this plea in the name of the "permanent prosperity of the city"? I confess that I am amazed that sensible business men should ever have offered it. But nothing ever occurred in this community so utterly disheartening as to have those hundred and fifty solid men stand up before our fifty saloons and, while widows and orphans, and wives and children more wretched than widows and orphans, and mothers heart-broken and prostrate under the brutal blows of inebriated sons, were pleading for the protection of the laws, say to those who have endeavored in a few instances to interpose by the authority of the State between this illegal traffic and its miserable victims, "Stand back! let those who will, enter these gates of death; we guard these portals, and in the name of 'general business,' demand that they be not shut. We pledge ourselves, against the law of the State, to keep open these avenues of death and hell. To those who would close them in answer to the pleadings of helpless women and children, we say, 'desist further action.'" I think I never endured a more sickening sensation than when I read the one hundred and fifty names attached to this petition.

The Action of the Council.

But what did the Council? It did, in some respects, better than the Opera House meeting or the one hundred and fifty petitioners had done.

1. It condemned the action of the hotels in closing their doors against the public.

2. It admitted that it had no power to license or protect the sale of intoxicating liquors.

3. It allowed the right of private citizens to make complaint of violations of the prohibitory law, and admitted that it was its duty to prosecute offenders.

4. It promised to enforce the law against all who might sell intoxicating liquors 1, to minors; 2, to habitual drunkards; 3, to persons to whom they had been notified not to sell; 4, to paupers.

5. It proposed to close up any saloon that might thus violate the law, upon the first conviction for the same.

6. It offered a thousand dollars for the detection and conviction of the incendiaries who burned the Imerson House.

7. It exacted from saloon-keepers $50 for the same licenses it had granted for $5 in the beginning of the year, each license to contain the following clause, to wit: "This license shall not be construed or understood as permitting or intending to permit, authorize, or license the sale of any spirituous, intoxicating, fermented or malt liquors, or beverages contrary to, or prohibited by the law of the State of Michigan."

The Council did, it is true, censure the prosecutions which had occurred, and adopted some other resolutions sufficiently inconsistent with the above. Indeed, an attempt was evidently made to please both parties, and as is usual in such cases, nobody was fully satisfied.

Masked Batteries of the Enemy.

I published an article in the *Times*, endorsing the action of the Council so far as it was worthy of endorsement, which was responded to by a writer over the significant *non de plume*, "Saloon-keeper." It is not necessary for me to speak of the style of this writer, only so far as to say that he seemed very much at home in the character assumed, using the language common to the profession with ease and fluency. He could hardly have done it better, if he had really been what he pretended to be. He denounces our present statute as "an illiberal despotic, sumptuary law," says that "our saloons will go on doing an orderly and respectable business;" says further, "We pay our money for the privilege of selling liquor under proper restrictions. The Council knows it, the citizens know it." * * * * * * * "We do not claim that the Council can amend the State Law, but we do claim, that in section 9 of an ordinance to amend an ordinance relative to licenses, that a saloon is defined to be a place wherein beverages or drinks, other than tea and coffee, are provided, or furnished to casual visitors, customers, or frequenters, and sold to be drank or used therein. We keep such places"

I will not defile this paper, nor this place with quotations from the gross personal abuse and misrepresentations of these articles.

Any one who has any curiosity to see them, will find them in the *Adrian Times* for August 2d and 4th, 1869. At a large public meeting, held at Odd Fellows' Hall, August 6, 1869, from which I was absent, these articles were pronounced by formal resolution unanimously adopted, as full of the most glaring misrepresentation and slander. In the publication of these articles, the writer secured a drunken alderman, who had not literary ability enough to copy them, to assume the responsibility of them, and he in turn employed the services of another drunkard to copy them, in order that they might not go to the office in the handwriting of their author. This may certainly be called anonymous writing; first assume a fictitious name and character, then secure a second person to be responsible for your articles, then secure a third to copy them, so they may not appear in the printing office in your handwriting, and then make the most gross personal attacks, without the least provocation, upon a man who writes over his own name, assailing no one, but merely commending what he deems right in certain public officers, and then make your boast that the authorship of your articles cannot be proven! What kind of a man do you think would be guilty of such a course as this? Would you expect that such a man would ever desire to have his name breathed among honorable men? When the name of this writer was demanded, his articles ceased. Would you believe me if I should tell you that this man is not and never was a saloon-keeper, that he professes to be a temperance man, and even a prohibitionist! It is even so, and should you meet him to-morrow, he will tell you he is as good a temperance man as I am. This man has been the great champion and mouth-piece for the saloons during our whole struggle, and no other ten men have done as much injury to the cause of temperance, or so encouraged and strengthened the dram-shop party as he. He seldom shows his hand, but strikes in the dark, and this Indian mode of warfare has been extremely effective against us. The day following the action of the Council, the saloon-keepers and hotels resumed their business. The temperanae men discontinued prosecutions for a time, looking to the City Council to redeem its pledges "to prosecute all known flagrant violations of the law." The City Marshall did circulate what was called a "black list" in all the saloons, forbidding saloon-keepers to sell to certain parties. Some two or three were prosecuted and fined for selling to drunkards and minors, but no saloon was closed by the authorities. One license was taken away, but another was immediately issued for the same saloon. The fifty dollar licenses were only partially collected, some paying only ten dollars, and some getting off with five.

The Incendiaries.

In the meantime detectives were keeping a sharp lookout for the incendiaries who had fired the Imerson House. Some of our officers were untiring in their efforts to bring the criminals to justice, and finally succeeded in detecting the man who had burned the building, and through him the two men who had hired him to do it. The man who fired the building was a worthless colored fellow, and the men who employed him were saloon-keepers at the time. All three were tried and found guilty, and sentenced one for one year, another for two, the other for five years to State Prison, where they now are suffering the penalty of their crimes. But were they the only guilty parties to this transaction? By no means. Both of the principal hotel-keepers were implicated in the testimony. One of them suggested the burning, the other came into court to swear one of the incendiaries clear, and was compelled the next day to make an affidavit that he had the day before sworn not according to the facts. It was also in evidence that a large number of the saloon-keepers contributed towards the paying for firing the building, but proposed not to know what they were paying for at the time. It did not appear in evidence that they did know what they were paying for, but who doubts? The truth is, the saloon-keepers in general were implicated in this transaction. Threats had been freely made before, and this was but carrying out their policy. Were the men who made the threats, and did nothing more, guiltless? Did they not encourage the incendiaries? What did they do but give form and active reality to these threats? Were the professed temperance men and church members, who denounced the law upon the streets as impracticable and odious, guiltless? Certainly they were not. They gave their moral support to the business of liquor-selling, and to the crime committed in its interest. Had professed temperance men and church members all stood firmly by the law, the liquor-sellers would have been overawed, and no violent opposition would have been made to its enforcement. No class of citizens so encouraged these vile incendiaries as some church members who championed their cause.

It came out in evidence on the trial that attempts were made to mutilate Mr. Van Sandt, the principal prosecutor, by throwing vitriol into his eyes, and from other facts in our possession, we have reason to believe that arrangements were made for his assassination on the night of the fire. It is certain that men were lying in wait for him between his residence and the Imerson House, but strangely enough, the alarm of fire did not awaken him, and therefore the plot at that point failed. I am told that there are facts yet to be revealed in connection with this matter which will implicate parties whom the public little suspect, and which will show the plot of the whisky ring to have been deeper and darker than was ever dreamed of by the uninitiated. My good friend, beware where you stand when the whole truth comes out.

Nothing ever did more for the good order of society and the enforcement of the law than the conviction of the incendiaries. The Court House was crowded to its utmost capacity with liquor sellers, sympathizers and temperance men, all anxious to hear the final charge and sentence of the judge. He delivered his charge in a very dignified and impressive manner, showing the utter futility of all combinations and conspiracies against the law of the land, and denouncing the hotel strike as an act of war against good men and a holy cause, as a contest of barbarism, lawlessness and vice against civilization, public order and virtue, which was entirely inexcusable. When the prisoners were sentenced every true man breathed more freely, and liquor sellers and their friends saw, as never before, the majesty of the law.

Failure of the City Council to Enforce its own Ordinances.

Still the temperance men waited for the Common Council, according to its pledge, to enforce the law against the saloons. But every day it became more and more apparent that it had no serious intention of such an enforcement of the law as would materially embarrass the sale of liquors. The work of moral degradation and death was still going on with unabated fury. New victims were continually brought to our notice, and the professed temperance men who had all along opposed us, seemed to rejoice in the reviving power of the saloons. But the real temperance men could not remain long inactive.

FINAL CHARGE AND VICTORY.

On the 20th of January a meeting was called at Odd Fellows' Hall, which resulted in the organization of the Lenawee County Prohibition League, under whose auspices, up to June 1st, 1870, forty-eight cases had been prosecuted, twenty-nine convictions had been secured for the first offense, nine for the second, six had paid costs and promised to go out of the business; in one case we were beaten, in one case the jury disagreed, but the defendant paid costs rather than try it again, two saloon-keepers prosecuted for the offense, " dug out," and thirty-seven saloons and dram shops had been closed in the county. The City of Adrian and Lenawee County owe a debt of gratitude which they can never repay, to C. E. Weaver, Esq., the late City Attorney, and to Justice C. B. Johnson, for the fearless, faithful and impartial manner in which they have performed their duty as Attorney and Justice of the Peace, under the severest pressure of threats of expulsion from office, and ostracism from their party, and intimidations of every possible character. Most of these cases have been tried before Justice Johnson, and I think it is the verdict of the whole community, that no magistrate ever administered the laws with an integrity more unwavering, or with a more scrupulous regard to the sanctity of the law, and to the rights of all parties. Mr. Weaver has exhibited marked ability as a lawyer, which those who have honest business with his profession will not be likely to forget. The prosecutions just now seem to be pushed with a little less vigor than usual. Why is this? There are two reasons. First, the want of funds to pay expenses. This embarrassment will always be recurring wherever the enforcement of the law is left to private individuals and to voluntary contributions. This should be remedied by an amendment of the law. But until this can be done, let us show our interest in public virtue by the liberality of our contributions for the enforcement of this salutary statute. Secondly, the day of political nominations is drawing nigh, and politicians are afraid of the influence of the whisky ring. The only question now at issue between the old political parties is, which shall secure the patronage and support of the whisky ring, and the corrupt masses of society! And both parties are vieing with each other in their efforts to secure this support. In order to this they are bowing down to whisky just as the old Whig and Democratic parties did to slavery. There is nothing that our great political parties will not sacrifice for votes. Therefore, when nominations and elections are pending, whisky is king, and temperance and virtue and law are below par. This state of things, of course, embarrasses to a greater or less extent the enforcement of the law.

LESSONS.

Now what are we to learn from this history? Has it any great lessons for us? We are to learn, 1st. That in the temperance struggle now before us, we are engaged in a contest with a powerful enemy thoroughly entrenched in the private, and domestic, and social habits of a large portion of the people, and having to an alarming extent control of both the old political parties, and though we have no doubt but the great body of the Christian churches is in heart with us, and when not controlled by fear or party prejudice, will act with us, and those who oppose us are generally as much out of harmony with the spiritual work of Christ as with the temperance movement; yet we are compelled to admit that our great enemy is not without influence and powerful agents, even in the most radical temperance churches. 2d. That legal prohibition of the sale of intoxicating liquors can be enforced in Michigan, in at least 47 times out of 48, which is as much as can be said of any other law upon the statute book. 3d. That incendiarism and mob law, when inaugurated in support of the liquor traffic, and to overthrow the authority of the State, though supported by men of wealth and position, can be suppressed by regular legal processes. 4th. That the prohibitory law enforced, even though it may not entirely suppress the traffic, will control, and regulate it far better than any license system can. It puts the business under the ban of the law, and condemns it by authority of the State, reduces the number of dram shops, and puts more restraint upon those that sell than any license system ever has done, or can do. 5th. That our law should be so amended as to give us a search and seizure clause, and provide for the appointment of officers specially charged with its enforcement. No law of the kind should be left to be enforced by mere volunteer efforts and voluntary contributions for expenses. As it is a measure for the highest public good, it should be sustained by the most efficient form of public support. 6th. That though there are good temperance men in both of the old political parties, yet since neither of these parties, as parties, are pledged to temperance or prohibition, they cannot be depended upon as politicians to enforce and sustain the law when nominations and elections are pending. There may be some honorable exceptions, but they are so rare that they are of but little practical value, and the only remedy for the failure on the part of our public officers to sustain the law, is in the support of temperance men in a temperance party, where they can have no motive or temptation to diminish their efforts in behalf of temperance for the sake of a nomination or an election. In a prohibition party, the firmer a man stands for temperance, and the more earnest in the enforcement of the law, the more popular will he be, and the more likely to be elected. Let us, then, act with the only party of principle, the only party in which a Christian man's conscience can remain inviolate, the only party that offers a reward for temperance and virtue, or even holds them at par. It may be said that such a party can never succeed. It can, and it will. We have a majority of temperance votes in this State to-day. They only need to be brought out and organized to carry the State at any time. This will take time, but it will be done. We had by count vote nearly twenty thousand majority twenty years ago. The question has never been fairly put in issue from that day to this. It will be, and we shall win. But, win or lose, I stand with the right. The old parties are wrong, the new party is right. I, therefore, repudiate the old and stand by the new.

www.ingramcontent.com/pod-product-compliance
Lightning Source LLC
LaVergne TN
LVHW011128110826
845150LV00008B/2278

* 9 7 8 1 4 1 8 1 9 5 2 4 3 *